This Land Is Our Land!

Reclaiming Our Heritage

by
James J. Dobranich, Sr.

1663 LIBERTY DRIVE, SUITE 200
BLOOMINGTON, INDIANA 47403
(800) 839-8640
WWW.AUTHORHOUSE.COM

First published by AuthorHouse 10/26/05

ISBN: 1-4208-7923-5 (sc)

Printed in the United States of America
Bloomington, Indiana

This book is printed on acid-free paper.

Table of Contents

PART ONE
Indian Heritage

Foreward

The citizens of this nation, the United States of America have, throughout our Nations relatively short history, shown themselves to be one of the most kindest and gentlest people in the world. On this matter, there is no doubt! Those who look back into our past, as related to the histories of other nations of the world, could only come to the same conclusion.

Not only have we shown our people to be most compassionate, they have also, because of their "Yankee Ingenuity," become the most progressive and productive people in all of mankind. This cannot be questioned or denied. As such, the United States of America has become and, in fact, is the pre-eminent Nation on the face of this planet.

Still, within our society, our country, there are those amongst us that would not only dispute this fact, they will claim otherwise. For what reasons—who knows? I do not know if this is an innate characteristic, among some of our citizens, for self-depreciation as well as nation-depreciation, or what. They seem not to be satisfied with accepting the good in our people, as well as the bad. No, we are not, as a nation or a people, without fault.

We are, nonetheless and for the most part, a most caring people. Our wars are usually not of our making but are fought in consort with others in order to provide democratic societies subject to the rule and control of its citizens and the needs of their people. In such wars, we have not been the aggressors or the conquerors. We have not been land grabbers, as many would like to portray us, neither on the Worlds stage nor within the founding, formation and building of this country.

This brings us to the fact that, in this day and age, many of the white race, still hold out our ancestors: the explorers, the pioneers, the settlers and such, to have stolen the land, now our country, from the Indians. This is simply not true! It is my intention to wipe this misfortunate impression, of our founders, our people, from our minds. YOU CANNOT STEAL FROM

SOMEONE WHO HAS NO ACTUAL, INHERITED OR DOCUMENTED

INTEREST IN THE PROPERTY, BE IT LAND OR OTHER MATERIAL

Chapter I
Our Indian Heritage

The Reader's Digest Book: America's Fascinating Indian Heritage, tells us that the New World, the America's, is a land without a truly "native" population. Also, the term Indians is in fact a misnomer. Columbus when he arrived in the Americas, in 1492, mistakenly thought he had reached the East Indies of the Orient, thus he called the newly found land Los Indios. As a result, they are still called Indians and are universally known as the American Indians. In a strange way, Columbus was partly correct, as their forebear's, it is believed, did in fact come to this land of ours from Asia.

As best, as it can be determined, it is shown that the Indians arrived in this land during the ice age, sometime between 12,000 and 18,000 years ago, via a land bridge between Siberia and what is now known as Alaska. This land bridge, the

'Bering Strait,' provided the means for passage from Asia to the Continents of the Americas. Some historians believed those that made this trip, to be of Mongolian Ancestry. In any case they were not explorers, settlers, or adventurers and were, in fact nomads following the game on which their livelihood depended. Their goal was neither to explore nor to settle, but merely to pursue/follow, the migrating animal herds, such as the caribou, for food.

When Columbus arrived in this land, the first people to migrate to this land the Americas greeted him. They were not an indigenous people to these continents but only the first immigrants to the New World. (There is, today, considerable evidence that others had preceded even Columbus to this land, such as Vikings.)

In the evolutionary theory, the first people to set foot here, those who followed as well as their descendants were, like all of us, Homo sapiens, having the same mental and physical capabilities. They were not, so to speak, out of the Stone Age. They, the Indians and the Eskimos—the last group to cross the land bridge—needed human reasoning and imagination. They had to have a remarkable ability to survive and overcome the many hardships they had to face, just to survive.

Although we mistakenly think of the Indians as a single similar people, they were, factually, as diverse as the Europeans. They were just like many other societies, consisting in great part of the rich, the middle class, and the poor. Still many of them did observe equlitarianism while lineage and wealth rigidly ranked some individuals. Even the Indians, it could be said, had areas where there was a hierarchy with absolute power, as well as having regions with a total absence of any centralized authority.

As earlier stated, the nomads who first came to this land from Asia, the "Indians" were not here to settle the land or even own the land. To the Indians, such a concept was incomprehensible; one could no more own the land than they could own the sun or the rain. With this fact embedded in their minds, the Indians who worshiped the land would therefore deny that they owned the land. They did not believe in land ownership.

For geographical purposes, the areas where the Indians lived are broken down into specific areas where the majority of them were located and actually encompassed the entire regions of North America in 1500.

The SOUTHWEST
The Five Civilized Tribes
The GREAT PLAINS
Nomadic Horsemen
The SOUTHWEST
Planters and Herdsmen
GREAT BASIN, CALIFORNIA, PLATEAU

Foragers and Gatherers
The NORTHWEST COAST
Traders and Fishermen
The SUBARCTIC
People of the Caribou
The ARCTIC
Dwellers in an Icy World

Additionally, there was what is known as the Lost Indian Civilizations--Kingdoms of the Sun-- as well as the Contemporary Indians--renaissance of an Ancient People.

In the year 1855, Chief Seattle of the Duwamish tribe stated: "There was a time when our people covered the whole land as the waves of the wind-ruffled sea covers its shell-paved floor. But the time has long since passed away with the greatness of tribes now forgotten. I will not mourn over our untimely decay, nor reproach my paleface brother with hastening it."

Although this quotation is quite elegant, it is not factually correct. At the time Columbus landed in this, the New World, it is estimated/believed that only about 10,000,000 Indians occupied the entire area of North America. North America coupled with Alaska, when rounded off, consists of 4,000,000 square miles, it is hardly possible to claim, in fact: "That the Indians owned this entire land." Put in another perspective, all the Indians of that time could have lived in an area the size of New

York City. Knowing this, would anyone be willing to cede the ownership of all lands encompassing the entire United States, to the Indians, now or at any other time in our history. In fact, one could rightly say that the Indians, for the most part, never set foot on much of this great body of land. Therefore, how could anyone with any knowledge of geography or with common sense, still claim that this land, the United States of America was once owned in total by, relatively speaking, a smattering of people.

Further, it can be shown that the "White Man" did not steal the land from the Indians. How could we have stolen it if, by any sense of reasoning, the Indians could not be deemed the owners of this land?

Also, they were not, as previously noted, settlers, they were wanderers or better stated nomads. They did not come here to settle the land, they came here by chance and, once here, to live off the abundance already provided by the land. As the abundance was limited/depleted, in a particular area, they merely packed up and moved on. They had no desire or reason to take possession of the land. They were, in fact, living off "The Fat of the Land!" Is it any wonder why they came, so to speak, to worship the land? If they were, at the time, learned in the Bible, they would have believed that they had arrived in the Garden of Eden.

Still there are those amongst us, perhaps the majority of our citizens who, to this day, would take umbrage toward anyone who would even suggest such a thing. How could anyone say that the Indians did not own this land/country? How dare they say such a thing? The question should be: In the light of today's knowledge, regarding this matter, how could they not say it. Fact is that one cannot lay claim to anything of which they have/had no rights to—like land they never even set foot on!

"Our duty is to preserve what the past has had to for itself and to say for ourselves what shall be true for the future."

Attributed to John Ruskin

Chapter II
Who was Really First

How new is the New World and who were the first people to come to this land, the Americas? These questions have not been, to this date, definitely answered. For Example:

1.   There are similarities between the cultural relics of the Far East and the ancient America's suggesting that, in the distant past, there were transpacific voyages to the New World. Might it be that the Chinese or Japanese were the first to arrive in this land?

2.   When the conquistadors arrived in the New World, they were amazed at the creative capacity they found amongst the native populations. Causing them to question just where this inspirational capacity came from. Was it from

Egypt, Phoenicia or, perhaps, even from Outer Space.

3.   Why has the Egyptian connection been frequently made?   Was it because of the many perceived similarities in relics found or were these coincidences based on wishful thinking?

The Europeans, upon finding/discovering this land, called it the "New World."   However, they, the Europeans, were late arrivals to these shores. In science it is now agreed, by most, that the first immigrants to North America arrived from Asia, via a land bridge.   Further more, recent evidence suggests that in South America, there were arrivals to this land as early as 30,000 years ago.   With additional knowledge, it has been suggested that an early arrival "time frame" for the first arrivals to this land could be established as sometime between 27,000 to 40,000 years.

Twentieth-century technology, notwithstanding, there is, scientifically, no single dating method that covers all human history.   We have used methods such as—dendrochronology, or tree ring dating, up to today's radiocarbon (carbon 14) dating, as well as others.

Each dating method has had its drawbacks! More recently, a new method called—amino acid racemization—is now used as a present day dating tool.   Since no single dating method can tell everything that needs to be told, for the time being, scientist must get their answers piecemeal.

Pre-historians are still considering new scenarios. Even to the extent that the early people might not or did not arrive in this land via an Ice Age land bridge. In 1968, pre-historians were turning up evidence that human occupation of Australia occurred between 25,000 and 30,000 years ago. Today, this date has been moved back to perhaps even 40,000 years ago, and some experts would take this back to 100,000 years ago or more. Further, it is believed that other arrivals/people crossed our continent at an earlier date and that they came by boat.

So the questions arise, if an early people could have reached Australia by boat, why then could they have not arrived in the Americas—the New World—the same way? This poses another question—were the early arrivals to our land, via a land bridge—the first and only ones to have migrated to this new land? If not, could it be that the others arrived here as early, if not even earlier, by other means, such as watercraft. This of course leads to still more questions: if the American Indians/Eskimos were not the first migrants to occupy this land—how can they be granted ownership or even claim ownership.

If they, the American Indians, owned this land, how is it that the Eskimos did not, on the same basis, acquire ownership to Alaska? Was it that

Russia did not presume that mere presence, by itself, constitutes ownership? Does this explain why our nation had to buy Alaska from Russia?

Using the above mentioned time gathering means/devices, it was ascertained that the total migration of the Indians and the Eskimos from Alaska down to the tip of South America occurred, from their arrival time, over a period of 11,000 years. Since their estimated arrival time into this area/land is placed, or determined to be, sometime between the years 12,000 18,000BC. If this is true, one might rationalize that the American Indians could also be considered late arrivals in certain areas of the Americas.

What are the facts supporting this contention? They are:

1.   It is well documented that many "Indian" people of various cultures such as the Toltec, Olmec, Maya, Aztec and the Incas populated South America. Each had their own distinct cultures/ societies as well as their different arrival period.

2.   There were remarkable similarities between the Cultural relics of the Far East and the Americas suggesting that perhaps there were also transpacific arrivals via watercrafts as well as land crossings. Could the Chinese or Japanese have been the first to arrive in the Americas? With my

limited knowledge of this subject. The Chinese Junks would, in such an early period, have been capable of such a voyage. In fact, this would, in my mind, apply to most Asia countries. However, they were not great sea powers. In the early part of the 15th century, china, in fact, limited its seafaring capacity.

Although the possibility of the Phoenicians being the true discoverers of America has many doubters, if I had to pick one as being first, I would support the belief that it was the Phoenicians. Although the evidence supporting this is dubious, it still gives some credence to the possibility, such as:

1. There is a map of the known world, executed in 1513 by the Turkish Admiral and cartographer Pin Reis. This map shows/includes a remarkably accurate rendering of South America's eastern coast. It is said that subject map was based on charts that were housed in the giant library at Alexandria before its destruction in 47BC. It is believed that the Egyptian mapmakers received their information from Phoenician sailors.

2. Additional Phoenician lore is that the Greek author Diodorus Siculus, who wrote in the 1st century BC that the Phoenicians had discovered in the sea beyond Africa "an island of considerable

size, fruitful, much of it mountainous…through it flows navigable rivers."

3. The Olmecs and Maya natives, like the Egyptians, wrote in Hieroglyphs developed a calendar and predicted the movement of the planets. Also, they built flat-topped pyramids looking much like the imposing Ziggurats of Mesopotamia and decorated them showing priests or rulers of Semitic aspect.

It is claimed that the Phoenician voyagers were the first from the Old World to discover the Americas. Also, today, it is believed that they were the first to sail around Africa. There is little doubt that they were the finest sailors of the ancient world. It is also known that the Phoenicians of Carthage sailed the Atlantic and another relic alleged to confirm a Phoenician landing in the Americas is the inscribed stone that was found at Bourne on Cape Cod, Massachusetts in 1658. As translated it read: "Hanno takes possession of this place." Hanno of Carthage was known to have sailed down the West Coast of Africa, in search of gold, in year 425 BC. However, it should be noted that this stone was deemed to be, by some, a hoax.

There is additional evidence that, inconclusive as it may be, could still lead to or add to the belief that they, the Phoenicians, might have been the first to reach these shores. Why is this important?

Well, relative to the claim that the Indians were the first to arrive in the Americas, it could serve to dispute such a claim and would deny them a right to claim ownership to any of the land, based on being first to arrive in this land. Still, this begs the question: Who were the first settlers?

"Believe nothing O monks, merely because you have been told it…or because it is traditional, or because you yourselves have imagined it. Do not believe what your teacher tells you merely out of respect for the teacher. But whatsoever, after due examination and analysis, you find to be conducive to the good, the benefit, the welfare of all beings— that doctrine believe and cling to, and take it as your guide." Attributed to Buddha.

Chapter III
North America in 1500

By the year 1500, the Indian populations in North America had become well established. Most of them had been living in the areas where they were found, by the newcomers to this land, for centuries. Looking at a map of the region, as determined by historians of today, throughout the 48 continental states—the United States—it shows that there were about 64 major tribal groups scattered throughout this land. Considering the vast area of the land, the small number of tribes of that period, they would have hardly taken up or occupied very much of the land.

In comparison with today's population they would have, relatively speaking, hardly shown more than a token presence and for the most part, left most of the land within the known area, untouched by their presence. In view of this, it is my contention that they, rightfully, could not claim ownership of much of this land, if any!

In the fertile lands of the East and Midwest, along some isolated pockets of the more arid Southwest, the Indians were, primarily, farmers as well as hunters and gatherers along with some fishermen. Along the Northwest coast and in some coastal areas some lived in settled villages. However, by and large, they consisted of nomadic tribes who built no permanent structures or even settled into a village lifestyle and governed their lives by movement of game and food crops provided by the land. This was particularly true of the tribes that lived in the Great Plains region.

Unlike the Indian populations on the eastern part of the continent, the populations of the Great Plains continued to change over several centuries, even after the Europeans arrived and established themselves as permanent residents of North America. These changes occurred, for the most part, because of wandering tribes looking for more environmentally favorable lands and by eastern tribes forced from their ancestral territories, by competing tribal groups. Yes, during this period, there was inter-tribal warfare.

Putting that aside for now, the question is what, if any, were their major and lasting contributions to this land. Well, aside from providing for their immediate existence, as well as those things they needed for their survival there is, from a major historical perspective, little of note. Contrast this fact, when compared with the major accomplishments, concerning artifacts, relics, monuments and cultures by the inhabitants of Mesoamerica—consisting of Mexico and the Central America—and of South America over a comparable period and you will find a measurable and remarkable difference in accomplishments. These facts have called into question as to who in fact was the first people to arrive in the Americas, and also by what means and routes did they come here.

Contrast the arrivals of the Conquistadors with the arrival of Columbus and in particular, when Bernal Diaz del Castillo of the day 1519 when he stood with Cortes and glimpsed, for the first time and in amazement, later wrote "…it was like the enchantments they tell of in the legend of Amadis, on account of the great towers and temples and buildings…" And some of our soldiers even asked whether the things we saw were not a dream…"

No such sights, apparently, fell on the eyes of Columbus and his men. Nor were there any proclamations made as to the great things their eyes were to behold. Perhaps they were in amazement at reaching land, however, they had no major pronouncements in regards to what they saw upon the land to cause them such amazement, as the conquistadors came to behold! Again, this calls into question: Was the entire Americas occupied by a single race of people and from one particular place?

If so, what can we use as a basis for the obvious major accomplishments of these people, in particular areas and lack of the same/corresponding accomplishments—in other areas of this land from people, supposedly of the same background and racial culture. How does one account for the major cultural difference/achievements between/within areas and continents of the Americas, if similar peoples as thought to be, founded this land?

Adding to the mystery is the lack of historical records that could date and document the growth of the Indian cultures. This brings to question: Did the early explorers and conquistadors come upon a transplant of Old World cultures? For hundreds of years now, it has been theorized that pre-Colombian visitors from Egypt, from Phoenicia, from Wales or from Scandinavia could have been the spark that ignited the development of civilization in the Americas. Regarding this matter, even amongst theorists of this day, their remains dissension. Relative to this subject I, personally, do not believe there will ever be one final answer to this question.

"Great nations write their autobiographies in three manuscripts, the book of their deeds, the book of their words and the book of their art. Not one of these books can be understood unless we read the two others, but of the three the only trustworthy one is the last." John Ruskin

Chapter IV
Tribal Wars – Plains Wars

In his book "Tribal Wars of the Southern Plains" Stan Hoig points out that: "Few people who cross the great American plains today remember that this land was once a warring ground. That here for centuries tribes fought one another for their own survival and then stood bravely against the irrepressible forces of white civilization. Even for those who are aware of its history, the Plains Indian conflict has largely been seen in terms of American conquest. Seldom has it been seen as the struggle of a native people to retain their homeland and way of life."

In the history of conflict and wars, it is almost always a "struggle of a native people to retain their homeland and way of life." However, one would have you believe that this type of warfare was exclusive to the Indian Nations of North America. War is almost always a fight to gain or maintain dominion/sovereignty of its land/country and way of life. There will always be such wars with good versus evil; depending on whose side you are on! Somehow, the Americans of today can only look at wars, such as the "Indian Frontiers" as a mean spirited war with the Indians being the good "guys" and the Settlers of this nation being the bad "guys". I am sure that if those of today that have such points of view were with the settlers of this nation, that their point of view might be different.

Long before the White man landed on this continent, the Indians were acting much like the White man and, for that matter, like all races of people. We have, for some self-deluding reason, allowed ourselves to be convinced that the Indians, throughout their history, were all peace loving people and hence they lived in a state of "Domestic Tranquility." Wrong!

Once again, one must go back to Stan Hoig's book to gain some additional insight and a better perspective on the life of the Plains Indian, before the intrusion of the White Man into/on their lands:

"For over three centuries of recorded history and undoubtedly much longer, the great southern plains of North America was a warring ground. During that period the region was dominated by bloody intertribal conflicts among the native tribes and their defensive wars against outside intruders…

Just as the whites had done throughout time in Europe and Asia, tribes contested adversaries for territorial rights, for captives, for property, for food and for the honor and glory of conquest."

"THE INDIAN FRONTIER OF THE AMERICAN WEST 1846-1890" BY Robert M. Utley gives us great insight into a conflict of people who were, it seems, destined never to understand each other. Further, his book is the story of, as stated: "this dramatic wide-ranging, multifaceted interactions between the 360,000 Indians west of the Mississippi River and American Soldiers, government bureaucrats, religious reformers, and an overwhelming number of white settlers between 1846 and 1890..."

Utley's book further points out that in recent scholarship that nearly ten million native inhabited North America in 1492. By the nineteenth century this population, the Indian population, decreased by more than ninety percent. These facts belie a false, but common belief of today, that the Indians populated the entire North American Continent and were pushed off the land by the invasion of the white man.

This is what many, to this day, still believe, that this continent was running over with Indians. It should be noted, for great many of the centuries that the Indians (Nomads) roamed this land, their means of transportation was by foot or over water.

The horse was not seen on this continent until the sixteenth century and the car, of course, much later. Prior to the advent of the car as our primary mode of transportation, and even with the trains, the average citizen of the time never traveled more than 20 miles from his home.

If this is so, and it is, then how can anyone believe that the Indians could have laid claim to all of this land? A total again rounded off, of about four million square miles. Additionally, these people were hunters and gatherers—not settlers. Yes, they worshipped the land, they wandered the land, they lived off the abundance of the land but they never laid claim to the land. No, not even squatter's rights. Even if they had made such claims, it would have been for very little of this land now called North America, that they could have laid claim to.

As previously stated, you cannot own that which you have never seen or even touched. If possession is nine-tenths of the law—they never met even this standard! And in the light of today's knowledge, they cannot, positively, claim rights to this land as its first inhabitants.

Additionally, throughout the land we now call the United States, it is recorded that there were only about 64 major Indian tribes. Placed in perspective, this would amount to just a little over one tribe per state. Hardly enough to have occupied the area of an entire state, let alone a sufficient number to lay claim to even a single state.

In respect to the plains wars, and in the totality of the Indian wars fought for this land, the number of Indians killed has been greatly overstated. In his book, "The SEVEN MYTHYS of GUN CONTROL," Richard Poe wrote:

COWBOY AND INDIANS

The worst violence in the Old West arose from conflicts between settlers and Indians. The death toll was high, yet probably lower than most people assume. "Although cowboy and Indian movies leave the impression that Indians were massacred by the tens of thousands, actual body counts show otherwise." To give just a few examples, anywhere from 170 to 600 Cheyenne may have been killed in the Sand Creek massacre of 1864, about 103 Cheyenne were slaughtered at Washita in 1868, 250 Shoshoni were murdered at Bear River in 1863, and perhaps 146 Sioux at Wounded Knee in 1890. Other massacres occurred, but these are considered some of the worst

"Taking all the army-Indian battles and massacres into account, probably no more than some 3,000 Indians were killed in the years 1789 to 1898..." "Settlers and vigilantes likely killed a thousand more." When we add the death toll from harsh living conditions and other mistreatments imposed by the white conquerors—such as the forced march of the Cherokees in the winter of 1838 – 1839, called the "Trail of Tears"—(it is) estimated that a grand total of as many as 25,000 Indian victims may have perished from democide by 1900. This is a large number but still hardly comparable to the death tolls in other countries."

In the book noted above, it goes on to state: "The biggest killer of Indians was not the bullets of the white man, but by his diseases. By some estimates, as many as 95 percent of the Indians of North, Central and South America may have perished from measles, small pox, and other epidemics brought from the Old World. This was a tragedy of unspeakable proportions, but it was not a democide."

Continuing in this vein, one of the biggest myths regarding this era, is that the White "Buffalo Hunters" of the time was responsible for mass destruction of the Bison. Again, this type of self-depreciation has lead us to a wrong belief. The facts, regarding this misperception are, as written in the book—The West, an illustrated History, by Geoffrey C. Ward:

"The history of the destruction of the bison has recently become more complicated than simple slaughter by the white hunters. The decline of the bison began long before the white hide-hunters arrived. Drought, exotic diseases transmitted by horses and cattle, competition with horses for critical winter habitat in the river valleys, increasing Indian population of the Great Plains, all depleted the herds before the hide-hunters administered the coup de grace following the Civil War."

In the battle for the control for this land, our land, it is good that the white man prevailed. Had the Indians won out, today we would be living in a much less prosperous country, and perhaps, even at the level of today's "Third World Countries."

"Where there is no vision, the people perish."
Proverbs 29:18

Chapter V
Indians – Our Foster Children

At the time Columbus arrived in the Americas, it is said that the white man stole Manhattan Island from the Indians for a few pounds of trinkets/beads. Although this story is not true, had it been, it would have been the white man that was ripped off—they paid the Indians to purchase land from them that they never owned.

Regarding Indian ownership of this land, John Quincy Adams surely spoke for his countrymen when he asked in 1802: **"What is the rights of a huntsman to the forest of a thousand miles over which he accidentally ranged in quest of prey? Shall the fields and valleys, which a beneficial God has formed to teem with the life of innumerable multitudes, be condemned to everlasting bareness?"** The obvious answer to the posed question is a resounding NO!

With the ending of the Frontier wars, the nations Indian problems were not immediately resolved. Only through much trial and error did the government arrive at a consistent program that could be called a policy. This policy was contained in: The Dawes Act of February 8, 1887. This was an act to provide for the allotment of lands in severalty to Indians on the various reservations, and to extend the protection of the laws of the United States and the Territories over the Indians, and for other purposes: Be IT ENACTED, That in all cases where tribes or bands of Indians had been, or shall hereafter be, located upon any reservation created for the use, either by treaty stipulation or by virtue of an act of Congress or executive order setting apart the same for their use. The President if the United States be, and he hereby is, authorized, whenever in his opinion any reservation or any part thereof of such Indians is advantageous for agriculture and grazing purposes to cause said reservation, or any part thereof, to be surveyed, or resurveyed, if necessary, and to allot the lands in said reservation in severalty to any Indian located thereon in quantities as follows:

> To each head of a family, one quarter of a section;
> To each single person over eighteen years of age, one eighth of a section;

> To each other single person one eighth of a section; and
>
> To each other single person under eighteen years now living, or who may be born prior to date of the President directing an allotment of the lands embraced in any reservation, one sixteenth of a section:

Sec. 5. That upon the approval of the allotments provided for in this act by the Secretary of the Interior, he shall…declare that the United States does and will hold the land thus allotted, for the period of twenty-five years, in trust for the sole use and benefit of the Indian to whom such allotment has been made…and that at the expiration of said period of the United States will convey by patent to said Indian, or his heirs as aforesaid, in fee, discharged such trust and free of all charge or encumbrance whatsoever:…

Sec. 6. That upon the completion of said allotments and the patenting of the lands to said allotees each and every member of the respective bands or tribes of Indians to whom allotments have been made shall the benefit of and be subject to the laws, both civil and criminal, of the State or Territory in which they may reside… And every Indian born within the territorial limits of the United States, who had voluntarily taken up, within said limits, his residence separate and apart from any tribe of Indians therein, and has adopted the habits of civilized life, is hereby declared to be a citizen of the United States, and is entitled to all the rights, privileges, and immunities of such citizens whether said Indian has been or not, by birth or otherwise, a member of any tribe of Indians within the territorial limits of the United States without in a manner impairing or otherwise affecting the right of any such Indian to tribal or other property...

Sec. 10. That nothing in this act contained shall be construed as to affect the right and power of Congress to grant the right of way through any lands granted to an Indian, or a tribe of Indians for railroads or other highways, or telegraph lines, for the public use, or to condemn such lands to public uses, upon making just compensation.

It is under such acts as above, and those that came after it, that caused the taxpayers of this nation to, in perpetuity provide the necessities of life to our native Indians. Further, to me, the Dawes Act leads me to question, if the Indians owned this land, somehow, they no longer maintained their ownership otherwise why would such an act be necessary so as to allot ownership of allotted sections of land, as proposed in subject act.

Yes, the Indians of today can truly say that they live off the—"Fat of the Land"—the hard working people of this nation who pay taxes that in turn are partly used to support our FOSTER CHILDREN— the Indians.

"The really basic thing in government is policy. Bad administration, to be sure, can destroy good policy, but good administration can never save bad policy." Adlai E. Stevenson

PART - TWO
Black Heritage

Foreward

Shortly after the Civil War this nation deemed it necessary, as well as desirable, to take action to insure that all of our citizens were protected in "Their Civil and Legal Rights." There were men in Congress who sincerely wished to protect the "Negro" in all of his new rights as a citizen (as opposed to a slave) and to secure for them political as well as economical equality. In order to do so it was felt that "An Act to protect ALL Citizens in their Civil and Legal Rights" be promulgated:

Civil Rights Act March 1, 1875

Whereas it is essential to a just government, we recognize the equality of all men before the law...

Be it enacted that all persons within the jurisdiction of the United States shall be entitled to the full and equal enjoyment of the accommodations, facilities and privileges of inns, public conveyance on land or water…

There is much more to the Civil Rights Act of 1875, however, my purpose in calling this Act to the attention of those who read this book is merely to show that even while our nation was in a state of "Reconstruction" we still could find the time to offer civil protection to all it's citizens.

However, down through the years, there were many and various ways that the Blacks of this nation continued to face difficult hardships and to be challenged in/by many various means; by those who would attempt to deny them full equality under the laws of this land.

After years of struggle and civil rights riots in the south, the Omnibus civil rights bill was passed June 29, 1964, banning discrimination in voting, jobs, public accommodations etc.

Today, the Blacks of America have "overcome" and are firmly integrated into America's society. In a relatively short period of time they have become, as a group, and when matched against any other group of blacks on this planet, the most prosperous of all. Most of the Blacks have come to this realization and, as one black said, he does not wake up, look in the mirror and see "Victim" scrawled across his forehead.

Yes, in the past, most of their ancestors had to suffer many indignities. However, today and for several generation back, there has been many blacks that, in fact, never suffered any hardships and prospered beyond their wildest dreams. Today, 67 percent of the blacks have attained compatibility with the whites. The others, those yet living near or below the poverty line are having their incomes supplemented by Government largess. They may not be well off, but they are, by far, better off than blacks within their ancestor's countries of origin.

Despite the above noted progress in their lifestyle, there are still those amongst the blacks that want to continually berate the white man and hold him, in effect, wholly and singly responsible for all their past ills. This is what I intend to address in the forthcoming chapters regarding slavery, the origin of it, factually, and race relationships, in general, in today's America.

Chapter I
The Slave Trade

Long before the discovery of America, slavery existed in Africa, West Africa and the Southern Savanna. African rulers often enslaved war prisoners, and the criminals housed in their jails were sold into the slave trade—often for shipment to distant lands and places where escape was less likely.

Many were exported across the Sahara to North Africa and sold to the Portuguese who were, briefly, in the business of buying slaves in one part of Africa and selling them in another part or area of Africa. This practice took place even before the demand from American plantations, across the Atlantic came into focus.

It should be noted that slavery in Africa was very different from the slavery on a plantation. A slave in Africa, immediately upon capture, was without rights and could be killed or sold, as his/

her captures desired. He/she continued without rights until sold to an ultimate master in Africa— or else to the Europeans for transportation across the seas.

However, in Africa, slavery was not only for the sake of money/wealth. For them the object was to increase the size of one's own group or for military power. Therefore, in many cases, women were more desirable than men. But men and women were assimilated alike, into the masters group. Another reason for slaves was to increase the groups labor forces.

The slave trade, across the Atlantic, as fact, tapped an existing African Slave trade, which, over the centuries, had existed sending its own people into a very different kind of slavery. Over time, it diverted increasing numbers to the coast for sale to Europeans. The organizations of this trade varied greatly from one part of Africa to another. Yes, even then the African slavers of their own people practiced a form of diversity.

The organizations of the trade varied greatly from one part of Africa to another. In some areas/ regions to Europeans even built forts where trading could take place. For example, 27 forts were built on the Gold Cost within 220 miles of each other. African authorities even allowed the Europeans to exercise sovereignty within the forts, charging them rent for the land the first were built on. On the other hand, other trading posts were nothing more than unfortified houses, onshore, for the storage of trade goods. These quarters also had tightly fenced yards to hold slaves awaiting shipment.

Whatever the point of trade, customary procedures already existed by the sixteenth century. Such trade normally preceded with a payment to the local authorities, which was, in part, a gift to the authorities, thus demonstrating good will and partly a tax. The internal trade to the coast was more diverse.

In some Kingdoms, (the term Kingdoms should not be equated to Kingdoms as normally understood) in the late eighteenth century, such as Dhomey, the slave trade was a royal monopoly tightly controlled for the benefit of the state. Other states, such as Futa Toro on the Senegal River, sold few slaves.

Well before the establishment of the United States of America, Europeans began to set up Plantations on the Atlantic Islands. Later, in the sixteenth century, similar establishments such as in the Caribbean and in Brazil followed these moves. North American, in fact, was never the major procurer/user of slaves. Regarding the slave trade into the Americas; Brazil and Argentina played a greater roll in the importation of slaves on this continent. Also, it was well known that these countries treated their slaves badly and in fact, worked millions of them to death.

Some form of slavery or forced labor was useful for other reasons as well. The natural conditions of frontier regions with plenty of land and few people were ready for the use of slave labor. For example, as the Indian population declined in Mexico and Peru, the Spanish turned increasingly to various forms of peonage. In Europe, the bonds of serfdom were tightened. The solution found for the Continents of the Americas, which consisted of numerous tropical lowlands, was slavery.

But Africans were not the only enforced immigrations to the New World. Convicts, unsuccessful rebels against their government and indentured workers who, more or less, bound themselves voluntarily to serve for a period of years were shipped off to the Americas in large numbers, especially to Brazil. Also, Indians were enslaved and used for plantation labor. However, of the sources of slave labor in the tropics, it was apparent that Africans seemed to have special qualities in this respect. As workers in such climates, they seemed to have superior abilities that were attributed to the Negro race, but modern knowledge of epidemiology shows that early environment as opposed to race, is the true explanation.

However, in this new trading community, West Africans played, almost from the first, an indispensable part of the history of their peoples as slaves, in other countries throughout the world. No one can question the violations that occurred in the slave trade. In this respect, the African Negro was paramount in enduring these transgressions.

However, all the transgressions were not by the slave buyers or plantation owners and, in fact, the sellers of their own people were guilty of some of the most heinous crimes against their fellow people. These facts, when discussing the slave trade, are seldom referred to in Politically Correct (PC) discourse. Still it must not go unsaid/unspoken. It is not only the white man that was guilty of such atrocities. It was equally, if not greater, among the African Negroes/blacks! As we now know, their black brothers, as a result of tribal warfare in many cases, first enslaved the slaves that were to be further sold.

It should further be noted that those captured in such warfare wee either enslaved in one way or another or, in far too many cases, they experienced despicable and merciless torture and, for many, death. In far too many cases, they were bled to death to obtain blood for various sacrificial and ritual purposes. For those who showed exceptional courage in battle, they would have their hearts cut out and eaten in the belief that they would, in this manner, acquire the courage of the one whose heart they would eat. Also, in many cases, their captives would, out and out, be cannibalized.

Yes, cruelty in the slave trade was a two way street. Their brothers/bloods that first captured them were in many ways, crueler to their captured brothers, than was displayed by the slave traders. Condemn one; you must condemn the others as well.

All the participants displayed these traits of cruelty equally. Still, in the present day history in many of the African Nations, slavery, in one form or another still exists and is being practiced. If the truth be known, the Hutu and Tutsi fractions of Africa killed more of their people in one year, as was killed in North America during the entire period of slavery.

For shear cruelty to its own people and in the present day, one need only look to the Nations of Africa, such as Ethiopia, Rwanda, Somalia and many others. And only recently, in southern Sudan, slavery has once again returned to Africa, where thousands of women and children are being taken into bondage. Until recently over a million people lived in a 30,000 square mile area of the Nuba Mountains—as written by Brian Eads and published in the Reader's Digest—what was once the home to some 50 black tribes, but after ten years of war, only a few of them remain.

What is happening in the African Nations of today pales by comparison to anything that happened in the past to the slaves on American Plantations.

Today, there is a lot of myth as opposed to fact, regarding slavery.

Myth: Africa was a primitive continent.

Fact: Africa was not primitive. If Africa were, in fact, primitive a large-scale slave trade would not have been possible.

Myth: America, or better stated, the white race was responsible for slavery.

Fact: A developed commercial slave trade/ network was already in existence in both West Africa and the Southern Savanna, long before the discovery of America. African rulers enslaved their war prisoners and then sold them into the slave trade for shipment to distant places such as across the Sahara to North Africa. In fact, the early African slave trade consisted of buying slaves in one part of Africa and selling them in another—long before the demand from American Plantations caused the internalized African slave trade to switch its focus across the Atlantic.

Myth: Most African slaves were transported and sold to plantation owners in North America.

Fact: Long before the founding of America, the European countries set up plantations on the Mediterranean Islands, southern Spain and Portugal. Europeans also established plantations on the Atlantic Islands such as the Canaries or Medeira. By the sixteenth century, they had included Sao Thombe in the Gulf of Guinean and in the Carribean and Brazil.

Myth: Africans, during the period of the slave trade were the only ones sold into slavery or enforced immigration.

Fact: Also convicts, unsuccessful rebels against their governments and indentured servants were shipped off to the New World in great numbers. Indians were also used as plantation slaves—especially in Brazil,

Myth: America's southern plantation owners purchased the largest number of slaves in the Americas.

Fact: North American plantation slave buyers, of the south, purchased about 20% of the slaves shipped to the Americas. South America—

particularly Brazil and Argentina—purchased almost 80%.

Myth: North American slave owners were the harshest and cruelest of the slave owners.

Fact: Slaves in North America, on southern plantations, were treated, in most cases, by their masters, to a life better than they would have had as slaves in other parts of the world—including their African homelands. In Fact, the great majority survived their slavery years in America. While in other nations, the great majority was worked to death.

Myth: The slave trade was allowed to exist because of the primitive conditions of African societies and the natural docility of these people.

Fact: Slave revolts were a common and standard feature—particularly in the Tropics of the Americas. Haiti was the first non-European country to overthrow colonial rule. Less known slave revolts were scattered throughout the backcountry of South America and the larger Caribbean Islands.

Myth: Africans were considered lazy people and only good for slave work.

Fact: They were highly valued for their ability to work hard and under hot tropical conditions.

Myth: Africa was not allowed to prosper because all of its good men/women were sold off in the slave trade.

Fact: Africa was not allowed to prosper because of its tribal diversity. It is stated that there were, at times, over one thousand African languages/dialects. Consequently, they could not, effectively, converse with each other. Also, because of this, they could not easily learn to read or write outside their tribal communities.

Myth: Africans sold into slavery were, supposedly, the cream of African society.

Fact: One could, in many cases, rightly say that they were the dregs of African society—it is known that many were sold into slavery to empty out their prisons. Also, many were captives of tribal warfare. As such, it could also be said that they were the losers from within their society.

Myth: African slave traders were not aware of the hazardous and terrible conditions that the slaves would be enforced to endure while being transported across the seas.

Fact: Wrong! They knew exactly what the conditions were and even prepared them for the journey by holding them in cage like conditions for several months and with little food and water or exercise, to better condition them for the trip.

"Not only do I pray for it, on the score of human dignity, but I can clearly foresee that nothing but the rooting out of slavery can perpetuate the existence of our union, by consolidating it in a common bond of principal." Attributed to George Washington

Chapter II
Race and Affinity for Africa

In their book "Africa-Africans" by Paul Bohannan and Phillip Curtin, it was noted: "Race, as a concept, is that it is based, in fact, on two concepts, they are: 1. Race has become the idiom in which it has cast some of its practices of and ideas about persecution and 2. Moreover, it has been utilized as a technical term by biological sciences and, particularly, by genetics. Thus, it has been assumed by the Western worlds that the popular idiom and the scientific concept have some bearing on each other."

"Race" as a social problem is what might be called a cultural displacement." Actually, the whole "race" question, in biological science, is a group of organisms that the members of which "statistically" significant proportion of their genes is reached for the purposes of scientists, in some situations/purposes to resolve problems relative to race. However, by gene counting, there is no point in nature at which one race can become another by virtue of having more or less genes common to a race. Race is part of the analytical process of science, not part of the data.

Races are the consequence of interbreeding populations. As such, they must meet in order to breed. Races must have a geographical dimension: an area in which it is represented or simply stated—interbreeding populations. As the interbreeding of present day races occurs with the breaking down of geographical and social barriers, new geographical isolation or new social barriers again create new interbreeding populations that a new set of races may result.

However, in the modern world, as defined in the dictionary race also means something else, that is: Race is derived from the Latin term for "root" and, also it has been used in English to refer to sex (the female race), to humanity (the human race) and additionally to refer to members of nationalities, religions and so on! Today, in the United States, of late, race is the revolutionary cry which new standards of equality and justice are being demanded.

In the United States, the monumental social changes that followed the Civil War (which occurred within a few years of the Darwinian revolution, though the results collided some decades later) gave rise to many of the present day beliefs about race in the United States. Not until after the Civil War, in America, is it that social problems that existed for almost two centuries are being expressed in an idiom of "race".

There is not, however, a clear line that can indisputably be drawn, or distinctions made that, unequivocally, can be claimed, that one group is Caucasoid and the other Negroid. In fact, among the most dominantly Negroid group, you can find Negroids with light skin and green eyes and in some areas of Africa; there are people with dark skin and kinky hair. In short, race is in the eyes of the beholder!

Until the 1770's or so, as a whole, in the Americas, more Africans, by way of the slave trade, were received than its total number of immigrants from Europe. This was especially true within the nations of Brazil, the Caribbean and Southern America. In these regions/countries and ultimately in Europe as well, Negro skin color, hair texture and facial features were associated with the status of slavery. Prejudices based on cultures and social rank were blended together and expressed as "racial prejudice." As a consequence/result, the basis of skin color came to be adopted. However and indeed, the classification of "human beings" by skin color goes back to ancient Egypt, even though the concept of "race" does not.

In America, throughout the debates about the abolition of the slave trade in the 1800's the Christians minimized similarities between Caucasians and Negroes to the most basic. The Christians claimed that Africans were "fellow creatures." However, a few would care to deny such an inconsequential claim. In fact, many arguments proceeded on rather or not the ""savages" were, in fact, ""naturally" inferior. Consequently, the stereotypes of the "Negro" began to appear in the great "chain of being" of which echoes were still being heard well into the twentieth century. Unfortunately, in some areas of the country, they still exist.

"Prejudices are rarely overcome by argument; not being founded in reason they cannot be destroyed by logic." Tyron Edwards

In the recent past, a poll was taken among the black that asked, in essence, this question: "With whom do you feel you have stronger ties—Africa or America?" I was somewhat surprised that the majority, 62%, said Africa. This leads me to question just where their loyalty lies, with the Nations of Africa or with the United States. It seems, since they were all born in this country, they should, as most people do, have strong feelings for the country of their birth—regardless of race or skin color. If they, the blacks, by now, do not feel that they owe their allegiance/loyalty to the nation of their birth when will they? After all, the Nations of Africa first enslaved its people and then sold them into the slave trade markets. How is it that they can have a loyalty to these very same nations?

Today, although one of the earliest of civilizations, African nations, by and large, are the poorest and most underdeveloped nations in the World. What is it that is so great about these nations that you would have strong feelings for them yet they have done nothing for you? Is it only skin color that matters? Seems to me that you asked only to be judged by your character and not by the color of your skin. Why the affinity for a country that, in essence, sold your people out. Are you saying that skin color does matter? That "whitey" is not your fellow countryman?

This I cannot understand, Africans in this day and age are still starving and dying by the thousands. Do their governments provide them with Welfare benefits, as blacks in America receive? My question is, what benefits do they provide you with. Hell, they do not even provide for their own citizens. Yet, the blacks, as a people/race, insist that the white man, either because of slavery or colonization is responsible for their present day lower status in life. Still a life that, by any standard of measurement, is far better and more advanced than any of their fellow black "bloods" in Africa would even dare dream of.

Today, just as some blacks in America blame their failures on the white man, the Africans blame theirs on the white Europeans – their former colonial "bogeyman", when, in fact, up until then, they had not shown any signs of progressive development. It was only after colonization that they, the nations of Africa, showed any signs of progress. No African nation, up to this point in time (the Fifteenth century), had even devised a written language, developed a calendar or had any concept of the biological origins of disease or learned how to domesticate an animal. Also, although they knew how to make iron, at this time; they had not, yet, made any mechanical device.

Far from holding the nations of Africa back, colonization brought economic development to them. It was the white European-Anglo Saxons who built the roads, the railroads, the schools, provided running water, communications facilities and so on, on the African continents. As of now, there is little evidence that Africans would have accomplished any of this on their own. Today we need only look to Haiti to readily see how well they, they people of Africa, (former slaves) left to their own devices, would have prospered!

Is it only that they are ready to bite the hand that feeds them—or have they harbored an inbred hatred for the white man down through the ages? I don't know what the answer is, but until we find out why there appears to be such hatred for a race that, in fact, has done as much and a whole lot more for the Negroes than they have for the white man or for that matter any other race of people.

As written in his book, Markets and Minorities, Thomas Sowell wrote: "One of the bases of claims for "compensation" or "reparations" to contemporary blacks for the enslavement of their ancestors is that the whites in general profited, even if they were not slave owners and even if their ancestors arrived after slavery was abolished." But if the baseline…is that baseline where these descendants would be if their ancestors had never been enslaved? …If that baseline is the difference between the average standard of living of black Americans, the grotesque conclusion of this arithmetic might be that blacks pay whites compensation…"

"May I tell you why it seems to me a good thing for us to remember wrong that has been done us? That we may forgive it." Charles Dickens

Chapter III
Black Racism

Not long ago it was stated, in effect, that blacks could not be racist against whites because there are more whites than blacks.

Well, we "honkeys" know better—don't we? There is black racism against the whites, but more than that, there is black racism against blacks as well as whites. If the truth were known, in today's world, blacks are more racist than whites.

You doubt this! Well, I suggest you talk to people of the Asian races. How about, for starters, the Koreans. Also, have you ever noticed that when they riot in the street, almost at the drop of a hat, it is usually the Asian stores that are hit the hardest?

However, never mind other races, the blacks have for political purposes, over all these many years, turned on their own people. Why, because these people—these black people—are not willing to say that they are inferior, that they can't make it on their own, that they need special privileges and so forth.

All my life, I have had the privilege of knowing many people of all races. They are, like you and me—only human. I know this sounds stupid, but what I am saying is that all humans are born (unless they are born dysfunctional) with the same needs and desires. Humans are not born or, by nature, lazy, stupid or mean. We all want to live and let live accepting what may come, but always striving to do our best.

I can honestly say, in my lifetime, I have met some of the best people, people not of my race, but that I enjoy as much in many cases, more than some of the people I have met, of my race—the white race.

What I am finding, in this day and age, is that many blacks are being misled to the extent that they are unwilling to accept the fact that they are not lessor beings. They are just as capable as any other race is to make it on their own. How, in this day and age, they can be convinced that they are not, is beyond my comprehension. In fact, I will not accept this premise. Look around you, if not in your own neighborhood, look elsewhere. There are millions of blacks that are making it on their own. Don't let anyone tell you that they are only making it because of "affirmative action, quotas or such." You are a great race; you are, so to speak, survivors. And I don't mean survivors of slavery. You are survivors because you can take the hard knocks of life and, yes, overcome them—as good and in many ways better than those of some other races.

But you are, unfortunately, listening to those amongst your own people that would put you down to lift themselves up. One cannot get more racist than that. Hell, if you can't trust your own people, whom can you trust? Yes, they will use the tried and effective means such as calling you an "Uncle Tom," if you happen to respect people of the other race or races.

Today, you are being led to believe that all "Cops" are out to get the black man. Not true! If the truth were known, blacks kill more blacks across this nation, in one year, than have ever been killed by the police.

Charleton Heston in a speech at the Harvard Law Forum said, "...A few years back I heard about a rapper named Ice-T who was selling a CD called "Cop Killer" celebrating ambushing and murdering police officers." He went on to cover this subject in a different vein. However, I would like to ask you, if you were a "cop" would you feel a little insecure on the job? Knowing that there are people who are just looking for a reason to kill you, and that songs/words are being spread, by virtue of supposed entertainment, encouraging others to kill cops? Would you, if you were a cop on the job, feel a little insecure and yes, a little quick to respond?

It is easy to turn your hatred on others. And this fact is well known to those amongst us that are "Race Baiters" and cop haters, regardless of their color. If you can hate all cops, you can, therefore, hate cops of your own race, for there are many in this category. And as such, in this case, it is black racism against fellow blacks.

In this vein, Mr. Heston went on, regarding more of the cop killers:

"…Every vicious, vulgar, instructional words:"

I GOT MY 12 GUAGE SAWED OFF.

I GOT MY HEADLIGHTS TURNED OFF.

I'M ABOUT TO BUST SOME SHOTS OFF.

I'M ABOUT TO DUST SOME COPS OFF.

Now I ASK YOU, AS A Police Officer, on the job, do you feel that these words might give one pause as to feeling secure in the performance of their duties. Do you think that, just maybe, if you were in this situation, that you might also feel a little nervous and yes, even scared, when a black man in the commission of a crime confronts you? How would you like to know that you have about $1/16^{th}$ of a second to decide to shoot or not to shoot? Remember your life is on the line as well as the criminals. In whose favor will/would you decide?

As you know, Jesse Jackson, as well as Al Sharpton are quick to judge others, particularly our men in blue. But do they do this in a rational way? No! It is done in a manner to insure they bring out the worst in many of us—racial hatred! Some still think that without someone to hate, they would have to accept blame for their faults. Yes, it is easy to blame others. Try it the other way around—accept/take personal responsibility for your own actions.

Ask yourself, why so many people of other races have come, races now numbering over 170 different nationalities, to this country. The downtrodden citizens of other countries, countries that they are willing to forsake everything, just to come to this country and to have a shot at making it on their own. Yes, if you can't make it in America—on your own—what makes you think you can make it on the poverty program?

Recently I heard a man, a black man, talking on TV to another black man—a black man with hatred for people of other races. This man in response to the others complaints said in effect: I don't wake up each morning, look in the mirror and see "VICTIM" written across my forehead. This man is a man! He will make it on his own. He will never be enslaved to any man, race of people or political party. He does not, and knows he does not have to, "cow-tow" to any person, place or thing. He is a black man. He is an American. For him, I have the deepest respect as I do for all others of his ilk. And there are many! How do I know this? Because I have met others of his race that are just like him. If they were not, I would not care what color they were I would still judge them by their character and not the color of their skin. Martin Luther King had it right. You can only honor him, King, by your actions and good intentions. You do not have to lower your character to appease those amongst us that would use you for their benefit—not yours.

Still among the blacks—African Americans—we are finding those in our midst that want to destroy the white man's heritage by attacking our founding fathers, our nations flag and yes, the confederate flag. Those people amongst us who seek only to divide the races for, I guess, some form of personal satisfaction or political gain are only now coming "out of the woods." Now admitting that they feel no loyalty to this country and, in fact, will admit that they will not say the "Pledge of Allegiance" to our flag. In effect, what they are really saying is that they do not have any loyalty for this country! As far as I am concerned, these people are in essence, truly "pimps." Yes, they will accept the fruits of this land, but feel no gratitude for it, in comparison with the nations of Africa, the bountiful life this nation provides to them. And these dregs of society would call our police "PIGS!" Yes, they dwell in the past finding only fault; just so that they can act out their "cry-baby" platitudes to appease their "wimpy" pygmy hearts! Let me just say to them, these people, these bushmen—you have no similarities to the blacks I have come to know that are, by comparison, Nilotic Giants.

"Perfect freedom is reserved for the man who lives by his own work and in that work does what he wants to do." Robin George Collingwood

PART - THREE
Spanish-Mexican Heritage

Foreward

Unlike the Indians or the slaves, the Mexicans of North America have a very strong link with Mexico and many of these citizens did, in fact, migrate/immigrate from Mexico to this country—the United States of America. In fact, many Mexican citizens of this country are direct descendants of those who have lived on the Mexican-United States southern borders at the time they were ceded by Mexico to the United States with the ending of the war between these two nations.

This war began on May 13, 1846, in response to an incident that occurred on April 23, 1846, when a party of Mexican soldiers surprised and defeated a small group of US Cavalry just north of the Rio Grande. The war between America and Mexico was finally ended when a treaty was signed on February 2, 1848, at the village of Guadalupe Hidalgo near Mexico City. As a result of this war, the United States gained more than 325,000 square miles of territory.

It should be noted the United States did not steal any land from Mexico. A war was fought and the vanquished paid a price. It should further be noted that although the ceded land belonged to Mexico, they paid little attention to its needs and the needs of its people living on this land. It is believed that had the American/Mexican war not taken place, as it did, the Spanish people living on the lands ceded to the United States would have, in time, revolted against the government of Mexico.

Down through the ages, since it's founding, the nation of Mexico and its citizens have, in one way or another, held clear lines of disrespect and hostility toward their neighbors—the Gringos. A historical review on the founding of Mexico and some of its relationships with its neighbor, the United States, will show that a continuous "state of belligerence" between these two people/nations has been present in their relationships. Even today, and among the Mexican/Hispanic citizens within our country and the whites, much of the past distrust and dislike, between these races and countries unfortunately, still exists.

Chapter I
Mexico – Mexicans

The Spaniards who conquered the Indians living in South Central Mexico during the first half of the 1500's first explored the area now known as Mexico. The Conquistadors (conquerors) had little interest in exploration and it is recorded, for the most part, that they thrived on personal greediness, cruelty and exploitation of the Indians of this region.

The most famous of the Conquistadors was Hornado Cortes (also spelled Cortez) who defeated the Aztec Indians in 1521. Cortes's military conquests led to 300 years of Spanish domination of the area now known as Mexico, as well as the West and Southwest parts of the United States.

Another famous conquistador was Francisco Coronado. From 1540 – 1542, he led his army on an expedition into the area (s) that became New Mexico in search of riches and gold. During this period, his men were the first to visit the Pueblo Indians of Acoma, Pecos and the Taos areas of New Mexico. They also traveled the Rio Grande and in addition, a group of his men were the first Europeans to reach the Grand Canyon.

Eventually Coronado was to lead his men south to Texas and north to what is present day Kansas. North of the Arkansas River in Kansas, Coronado found settlements of the Quivira Indians but still no gold and riches. Disappointed, he returned home to Spain. After arriving home in 1546, he was accused of committing cruel acts against the Indians in his army, but was found innocent of the charges.

From the 1500's to the 1820's, in an area known as the "Spanish Borderlands" in North America, Spanish missions established themselves among the Indians. This area, the Spanish Borderlands, extended from Texas, New Mexico, Arizona, California, Utah, Nevada and parts of Colorado and Wyoming. These missions became the home to many thousands of Indians, and at first, the Indians welcomed the many presumed benefits; however, all too soon, various problems developed.

Many of the Indians objected to the highly structured mission routine and to the fact that they were forbidden to leave without permission (much like slaves). Also, they resented the attacks by the missionaries on their religion, traditions and, most of all; they feared the disease that killed them by the thousands.

It is claimed that more Indians were killed during this period by the "white man's diseases" than in any other period of history, including the North American Indian wars. Further history shows that the native Indians taken in by the missionaries were eventually to realize that the supposed benefits were far outweighed by the misery that was to follow.

History shows that the unsettled conditions in Mexico, down through the years, presented the United States with various problems. This can best be shown/understood by a "Time Line" review, primarily, of the 19th Century, showing many of the reasons why a state of continuous belligerency developed between these two nations:

1823 – Mexico becomes a Republic.
1828 – Liberal revolt in Mexico, Vincente Guearrero becomes President.
1829 – President of Mexico overthrown by Gen. Anastasio Bustamante.
1833 – General Antonio Lopez de Santa Anna becomes President of Mexico; country threatened by Civil War.
1835 – Texas declares its right to succeed from Mexico.

1836 – After the battles of the Alamo and San Jacinto, Texas wins independence from Mexico.

1844 – Military Revolt in Mexico, Jose Joaquien de Herrera is head of Military Administration.

1846 – Negotiations between Mexico and U.S. for purchase of New Mexico fail in April; U.S. troops move into disputed area, defeat Mexicans at Palo Alto, formal declaration of war by U.S. follows; U.S. forced move into Santa Fe and U.S. annexes New Mexico in August.

1848 – Treaty of Guadalupe Hidalgo ends Mexico – U.S. war in February; ratified in October U.S. gets Texas, New Mexico, California, Utah, Nevada, Arizona and parts of Colorado and Wyoming from Mexico in return for large indemnity.

1863 – French capture Mexico City and proclaim Archduke Maximilian as Emperor.

1864 – Maximilian accepts and is named Emperor of Mexico.

1867 – Napoleon III withdraws his support for Maximilian and Mexico. French troops leave the country, Maximilian executed.

After Mexico's Revolution, which followed the above and with his election, President Woodrow Wilson in a Forth of July speech, 1914, presented his Mexican policy with compelling force. In this latter connection he said:

"You know...what a big question there is in Mexico. Eighty-five percent of the Mexican people/citizens have never been allowed to have any genuine participation in their own government or to exercise any substantial rights with regard to the very land they live upon. All rights that man most desires have been exercised by the other 15 percent..."

To me, the above partial quotation could somewhat describe the conditions in Mexico, as they exist today!

"The most important office...that of private citizen." Louis Dembitz Brandeis

Chapter II
Mexicans vs Whites

At the beginning of the 20th Century, Mexican-American problems continued to exist. These problems were further exacerbated when a destructive raid upon Columbus, New Mexico, by Poncho Villa, March 9, 1916, marked a series of affronts on the United States forcing President Wilson to send a punitive expedition force into Mexico under the command of Brigadier General John J. Pershing. This force failed to make contact with the forces of Villa and the last of the American forces were withdrawn from Mexico on February 5, 1917.

From the earliest times of the 20th Century, the Mexican and Gringo dislike, if not outright hatred for each other, continued to flourish. With the advent of World War II, there seemed to be a coming together between these two groups, if for no other reason, to fight to defeat the enemies of our country. The Mexicans, although a smaller group of citizens, served this nation well and with valor. Unfortunately, with the ending of World War II, the lines of dislike and distrust between the Mexican citizens and the whites of this nation once again reared its ugly head. And one could even say that the hatred for each other grew in intensity. This situation continued, in many ways, to exist until the Civil Rights Act of 1964.

With the Civil Rights Act, a case of forced integration became prevalent throughout the land. At first, it seemed, it was not working and many felt it was having a dilatory effect on race relations. However, with time, and with the races more and more coming together and getting to know each other better, racial harmony was more and more looking like a reality.

Still, it appears that with the renewed leadership of the Mexican/Hispanic community, race relations were once again being "stirred-up" this time for special rights and political gain. LULAC, RAZA UNIDA and other groups of this ilk were crying out for things such as bilingual education, more acceptances of illegal immigrants and so on. These special demands were in great part cause for the resurgence of dissension between the two groups of citizens to again rear it's ugly head.

As the Mexican/Hispanics of this nation continued to gain political clout on the national scene, the Democratic Party started to, more and more, court and recruit them into their political party. They, in turn, responded to this courtship and today they are, in fact, a major part of the Democratic constituency. So much, so that it was transparently obvious that Al Gore could not win the presidency without their support.

Their political clout was further demonstrated, as pointed out in the Los Angeles Times published on April 12, 2000, that: "…Gore's endorsement, on behalf of the Clinton administration, of an obscure house bill that makes illegal aliens living in the United States eligible to apply for legal residency if they are of "good moral character," and have lived continuously in this country since 1986."

Yes, the Democrats were so eager to gain the Hispanic vote that they, in fact, were willing to increase their numbers in blatant violation of federal law. In doing this, and to serve a purely politically motivated purpose, the Democrats to further appease the Mexicans/Hispanics were willing to violate the laws of this land.

Today, the Hispanic leadership will attempt to justify the illegal migration of Mexicans/Hispanics across our southern borders, by claiming that these illegals serve a legitimate need—cheap labor. This seems to me a contradiction of the parties' political platform, which is to advance the Labor Movement through higher wages. Why are they now claiming this country needs cheap labor? Also, they claim that they, the illegal aliens, pay taxes. Not so—cheap labor means low income and those on the low wage spectrum do not pay taxes. In fact, they may be getting, through Earned Income Credits (ECI) money from the government. This, in addition to all the other citizen benefits derived from the TAXPAYER'S, through government largess.

Additionally, with the continuous assault by illegal migrants of our borders from, particularly, Latin America and well as Asia and Africa, the face of America is rapidly changing. What are still nations of mostly European descendants' will, all too soon become a nation of mostly Latin, Caribbean and Third World people. And why are they deserting their own Nations? Because their homelands are failures, unable to serve their people with even the basic necessities of life. Because of this, they are now fleeing their countries to enrich their lives in the land of plenty—the United Stated of America.

Yes, these immigrants, unwilling to stay and try to change the face of their countries of origin are now flocking across our borders. As a result, we now have to ask ourselves—what is the future society of America to become? If those flocking to our shores, illegally, continue to do so, can we expect them to produce for this country? We have never had this kind of diversity nor has any other country. If we allow this migration to continue unchecked, by the time the toddlers of today reach middle age, the former founders and builders of this country will find themselves a member of a minority group—the white race!

Yes, we will become a minority within our own country. No other nation on the face of this earth would let this happen. This is to willingly provide over the attack on our people and to surrender our country—to a class of people (s) that had nothing to do with its making. Yes, we are a land of immigrants, but they came here legally and, for the most part, at a time when our nation was still in its infancy. As such, they assimilated into the national fabric of this nation and contributed to its making. They did not come here to eat at the trough of plenty provided by the labor of others. If they really were serious, they would get in line like all the others wanting and waiting to come to this country.

A column in the Middle American News read, in part: "…Immigrants are already a potent political force in elections and legislation. As ethnic advocacy groups and their political allies organize those foreign populations, America's heritage of individual liberty is being dismantled in favor of group rights, racial quotas and multiculturalism.

So far, the result has been overcrowding, environmental degradation, stagnant wages, ethnic conflict and radical political change.

Unless America reversed course soon, the identity of the U.S. will be permanently altered..."

And who is seeking political advantage by supporting this taking over control of our nation— the Democratic Party. If you doubt this, ask yourself, what is the make-up of their constituency. And to make matters worse, by the middle of this century, if the present trend is allowed to continue, the Hispanics will be 25 percent of the population. Couple this with the blacks being 13 percent and the soon to be 14 percent Asian population, they will not only become a major part of this country, they will dramatically change the color of the American citizen. Yes, white will be on the way out—colored's will have the political clout. Think about it. Will this be all for the good of the nation or will it be a destructive force.

"No democracy has ever long survived the failure of its adherents to be ready to die for it... My own conviction is this, the people must either go on or go under." David Lloyd George

Chapter III
Characterizing the Mexican

By and large, the Mexican citizens of this nation that were either born here, or legally came to this country and became citizens; are honest, hard-working, family oriented and religious people. They are also fun-loving, happy go lucky people whom, once your friend, you have a friend for life.

Given the above characterization, I ask myself, why are they, in a great majority members of the Democratic Party? Everything in their character, way of life, indicates to me that they are, as a race, more suitable to the ideas expounded by the Republican Party:

1. They believe in strong family ties.
2. They do not believe in birth control— have 3.5 children per year as opposed to 1

child per year for each other races. And, apparently, they are opposed to abortion.
3. Most are Christians and therefore are more attuned to the "Religious Right."
4. They are an exceptionally loyal race of people to God and Country.

So why is it that they join an organization that, for all the above reasons, they are in disagreement with? To me, that only means one thing—they want something (s) that the Republican party will not concede or give them and the Democratic party will. These wants/desires are:

1. Bilingual Education.
2. The right to a two-language country speaking Spanish and well as English. They do not want to give up their supposedly native tongue—even though, for the great majority, they were born into an English only nation.
3. They want the immigration rules changed to make it easier for the Mexicans/Hispanics to come to this country, as opposed to all other groups. Also, they want the illegal Mexicans "sneaking" into this country to get special treatment.

Looking at the above, each desire, when scrutinized has a singularly selfish or political motivation:

1. They do not want to assimilate into the American society, as the other 170 or more races of people that have migrated to this country are willing to do. One of the main reasons for this desire is, they say, to keep their heritage.

2. Bilingual Education is a crutch that their children cannot learn unless they are taught in Spanish.

3. They want this nation to give/allow their race a disproportional number of their people into this country that would, in the long term, give them, their race, additional political power—particularly at the ballot box. They are, plain and simple, looking for more control over how this country is run. In short, they are seeking additional Political Power.

To support the above positions, which are made to clarify the Mexican/Hispanic motivations, the following is provided:

IMMIGRATION FACT SHEET

In 1965, President Johnson quietly signed into law the "Immigration Reform Act" which overturned America's traditional immigration policy and replaced it with the most liberal, easy-access immigration policy in our history. As a result, nearly one million immigrants now legally enter our country each year, plus unknown, but large, numbers of illegal aliens. Opinions differ as to whether this is good for America. But all agree that this massive influx of unrestricted immigration is radically changing America in almost every way. Still, the politicians have yet to seriously address the issue of immigration policy and its ramifications for the future of this country.

Americans for Immigration Control, Inc., (AIC) is widely recognized as the leading organization in the country working to make politicians face honestly and openly the full impact and consequences for the "open immigration" policy – some of which include:

ETHINIC BALANCE. U.S. census projections indicate that if we stay on our current course, within 50 years our population will nearly double; non-Hispanic whites will account for less than half of all residents, and English will no longer be our clear and predominant language.

ILLEGAL ALIENS. The 2000 census revealed as many as 8.7 million illegal aliens now live in our country -– far more than ever disclosed previously.

TAXES. Services for immigrants, legal and illegal, cost taxpayers a record $68 billion per year.

SCHOOLS. Bilingual education doubles the cost of alien schooling with schooling of immigrants costing an average of 905 dollars more per family. And classes are swollen to where, in some parts of this country, they would need to build a new school a day just to keep up with the influx of immigrants.

ENGLISH LANGUAGE. The use of English as America's primary language is under assault – with everything from driver's licenses, voting ballots and even citizenship ceremonies now being offered in dozens of foreign languages.

CULTURAL IDENTITY. Our pride in Americas heroes, history and achievements is being undermined and replaced with an ethic of political correctness, self-criticism and the view of America as an "Oppressor nation."

SOCIAL SECURITY AND MEDICARE. 400,000 foreigners now collect SSI benefits from the Social Security Administration without having to work one day in America. And Immigrants get

Medicaid benefits 64% more often than the Native Americans.

JOBS. Cuba-born economics professor George Borjas shows that immigration cost the U.S. born workers $133 BILLION a year in job losses.

TERRORISM. In just one day (9-11-01) legal and illegal alien Muslin terrorists took the lives of approximately 3,000 people in New York, Washington, DC and Pennsylvania and destroyed tens of billions of dollars of property.

CRIME. Over 25% of today's Federal prisoners are immigrants. And in some areas 12% of felonies, 25% of burglaries and 34% of auto thefts are committed by illegal aliens.

WELFARE. Immigrants are 50% more likely to get welfare than natives – with a full 75% being more likely to get food stamps, medical benefits and housing assistance. Non-citizens now collect nearly $7 BILLION a year in benefits.

OVERCROWDING. Two-thirds of our population growth is due to immigration. And our cities, schools, highways, national parks, beaches, natural resources and even our water supply are already straining under the mounting pressure.

How many of these problems have yet to manifest themselves in your community? How concerned that your area will be adversely affected by the decisions politicians are making – without your knowledge and approval – regarding this highly controversial issue?

Our generous immigration policy encourages foreigners to exploit every loophole to get in. For example, more and more pregnant women sneak across the border so their babies will be legal citizens and open the door to their families and welfare. Some even "rent" children as passports into America. And elderly relatives of immigrants are brought in to take advantage of our Social Security literally using America as a free deluxe retirement plan for the Third World.

Most of the policies that have allowed for these practices have been put in place behind closed doors with little, if any, public debate or exposure.

"Every man among us is more fit to meet the duties and responsibilities of citizenship because of the perils over which, in the past, the nation has triumphed; because of the blood and sweat and tears, the labor and the anguish, through which, in the days that have gone, our forefathers moved on to triumph." Theodore Roosevelt

If those of us in this day and age fail to stand and defend what has been given to us by our forefathers, we may, perhaps, live to see our own grandchildren classified, as a minority in their own country—is this to be our legacy to them.

We are now facing an internal attack on all that our forefathers gave us—if we stand by and let those who would take advantage of our people for their gain we will, all too soon, come to rue the day we were born.

"Civilization, in the real sense of the term, consists not in the multiplication, but in the deliberate and voluntary reduction of wants." Mahatma Ghandi

Chapter IV
The Good, Bad – The Despicable

In the 2000 campaign for the presidency, Patrick J. Buchanan on April 28, 2000 made a speech that was so powerful that the "Corporate, Liberal Media" blacked it out. The titles of this speech and excerpts from it are:

TROUBLE IN THE NEIGHBORHOOD
"...Today, I fear America and Mexico may be headed for a time of trouble...Why do I believe U.S.-Mexican relations are headed downhill..." He continued with the following facts:

1. The Mexican army incursions, in the past five years (now 7 years) according to the State Department were 55. Recent incursions would put this figure at a higher

rate. In fact prior to his speech, he states: "...two truckloads of Mexican soldiers barreled through a barbed wire fence pursed a Border Patrol vehicle and two officers on horseback and fired two shots..."

2. "...As for the millions of illegals who have already entered this country, they have caused a demographic sea change. California has 34 million people and, if the border is not secured, will have 50 million by 2010. One-third of California's population is now Latino."

3. "...In 1998, the Mexican consul general in California exclaimed: "Even though I am saying this part serious, part joking, I think we are practicing La Reconquista in California."

4. "...In 1997, President Zedillo said: "I have proudly proclaimed that the Mexican nation extends beyond the territory enclosed by its borders and...Mexican migrants are...a very important part of it."

5. "...In February 1998 the U.S. soccer team played Mexico if Los Angeles' Coliseum. The crowd booed our national anthem. Fans who applauded the U.S. team were pelted with fruit and cups of beer. The U.S. players were showered with debris and spat upon as they left the field—in their own country."

6. "...The Latino student organization MechA openly demands return of the Southwest to Mexico. Charles Truxillo, a professor of Chicano studies at the University of New Mexico, says the creation of a new 'Aztlan,' with its capitol in Los Angeles is inevitable, and Mexicans should seek it by any means."

7. "...Ricky Sierra of One Stop Immigration declares: We're re-colonizing America so they're afraid of us. It's time to take back what is ours."

8. "...One demonstration leader in Westwood was heard to say, 'We are here...to show white Protestant Los Angeles that we're the majority...and we claim this land as ours. Its always been ours and we're still here...if anybody is going to be deported it is going to be you." (The statement is obviously made out of ignorance—In 1845, Californians did not consider themselves Mexicans but Spaniards).

Buchanan stated it best and loud and clear: "We cannot allow to rise within our country a nation where Spanish is the language and anti-Americanism the ideology."

We must never forget that within the Mexican community there is still hatred by some for the Gringo. They, like others, think we stole the land from them. Somehow, they cannot come to the realization that a war was fought—the United States won it and Mexico ceded the land to the U.S.A.

While we are on the subject, there is also another class of Mexicans within their race that are called "Coyotes." Of all the Mexican people, these are the most despicable—bar none. These are the Mexicans who traffic in the human misery of their own people. They are the scum of the earth! As explained by one, who knows, it was proclaimed: "The human traffickers frankly speaking, don't care about us, cheating on us to make money – later they abandon us in the desserts."

Down through the years, this scum of a human being has even abandoned some of those who they were supposed to be helping to cross the border when it appeared to them that they might be caught. In many cases, many were left behind and, on their own, died in the blistering desert sun or suffocated locked in abandoned car trunks or trucks.

What kind of people are they that they would trade in human despair? Not only that, but doing it to the people of their own race and who came to them for help only to find betrayal and death. These cowards, these dregs of society would also turn on their own country for money. Now it is being reported that they are helping terrorists to enter our country in order to rain havoc on this nation. I, for one, will never understand anyone, any race that would willingly sell out his or her nation.

Perhaps the answer lays in the fact that, just maybe, they want to see our nation destroyed to appease their ignorance and sick minds. We must never forget, and as sorry as I am to have to say it, among the Mexican citizens of this country dwells an innate hatred for the white man. This can no longer be denied. Yes, they may be few in numbers but it only takes a small number of such to do great harm to this nation.

Any citizen that would help bring into our country avowed terrorists intent on doing us harm has no love for this country, and given the chance, they would turn on us in a minute. We are now a nation that must be weary of our friends as well as our foes. This, we must never forget!

"The penalty good men pay for indifference to public afairs is to be ruled by evilmen." Attribted to Plato

PART - FOUR
American Heritage

Foreward

Since the civil Rights Act of 1964, it is evident that the Mexicans/Hispanics and the blacks wanted more than Equal Rights. It is now obvious that, for many, they wanted much more. Like special/ additional rights! Rights over and above what the races of others, the other 170+ nationalities within this country, ever got and they never asked for.

At no other time in our history have two races, because of the past perceived and real injustices they had to endure, are now being catered to by our political lawmakers. Has this appeased them— no? Each time we give them something, they find something else to want. They, one could say, have developed an insatiable appetite for more and more. Like a blackmailer, once the "sucker" takes the bait—he is hooked for life.

This appetite is constantly being encouraged by the likes of Jesse Jackson; our nations number one, in my opinion, blackmailer. Also, Al Sharpton, the nations first real, according to a recent picture, "Drug (Store) Cowboy." The NAACP has become a joke. We now have ex-cons, many of them calling themselves "Black Panthers" parading up and down our streets acting as if they own the country already.

Yes, we have street riots, dope peddlers, drive-by shooters, gang-bangers, and welfare queens, un-parallel numbers of children being born out of wedlock, and so on. And this is just to mention a few. And of course, it is the white man that is the cause of all this "crap" now prevalent and running rampant across this nation.

In addition, although these two races of people account for the majority of crimes being committed in this country—they, their leaders, are continually attacking our men in Blue who must daily face this wave of crime. Most of these crimes being committed by members of their own race on their own people. Sure, from time to time we see some abuse of power by law enforcement. However, seldom it is shown, in direct proportion, the viciousness being perpetrated by the thugs roaming our streets. In the year 2001, I have heard that over 56,000 law enforcement officers have been injured, many of who were killed, in the line of duty—where is the outrage?

Coupled with Liberals down-playing the Heritage and History of this country, in the classroom and the media, they think that they, in fact, founded or built this country and that, somehow, the white man took it away from them.

I hope that within the pages to follow, I will shed some light on this matter. It will be factual and, I hope, informative. In any case, it will show whom the real/true owners and builders of this country were and are—THE WHITE MAN!

Chapter I
This Land is Our Land
"Period"

We know that the Indians came to this land as Nomads, the Spanish as Conquistadors (conquerors and seekers of gold) and the Blacks as slaves. It was the Pilgrims, the Anglo-Saxons that came to this land with the full intent of settling here.

With their arrival, the Pilgrims immediately took responsibility for themselves and began to work and settle the land. For all practical purposes/reasons, they were our Nations first "Homesteaders."

It can be factually established that it was people of the White Race who became the founders of this Nation. It was the Pilgrims, those English and religious puritans, who founded the first colony at Plymouth, Massachusetts in 1620.

1. It was all the white men who, by signing the Declaration of Independence, placed their lives, their fortunes, their sacred honor on the line and, as such, they are considered to be this nations founding fathers.
2. It was the Revolutionary Army, under the command of General George Washington that fought and won for us, our nations independence. With few exceptions, this army was primarily composed of all white men. There is no other group or race of people on the face of this planet that can make this claim!
3. It was George Washington that became our nations first President and is considered to be the father of this country—no one can question this fact.

This is, in part, our history/heritage—we will not be denied/deprived of it no matter how much others will try to re-write it to pursue their own agendas.

It was the white man who, for the most part, became our nations explorers, pioneers, settlers and eventually homesteaders, and as such the builders of this nation. It was the white man, in the building of this nation, who stood at the forefront of:

1. The Mining Frontier.
2. The Cattleman's Frontier
3. The Farmer's Frontier

Yes, the Great West brought forth the existence of the free land. Land that was for the first time, to be effectively utilized, resulting in the colonization of the Great West and the advance of American settlements westward.

It was, once again, the white man who was at the forefront of Industry, Transport and Finance during the years 1865 – 1890. In 1860, America ranked fourth among the nations of the world in manufacturing; by 1894, it was first. By 1914 our nations industrial output exceeded the combined totals of England, France and Germany.

With the coming of the railroad it, by the year 1890, consisted of 156,000 miles of rail, enabled the country to forge ahead. With the advent of the Civil War, the long debated need for transcontinental railroads took on a new urgency. And the transcontinental railways soon took their place in our history.

At the forefront of the Industrial Revolution we, once again, find the white man leading the way.

The new technology coupled with oil and steel sped up the growth of this nations Industrial complex. Taken as a whole, all the aforementioned were the ingredients that made this nation a giant among nations, unsurpassed in its productivity as well as in it's freedoms and humanity.

The two major World Wars were fought and won only after America's intervention and participation in them. Yes, we have sent our boys; primarily white, to protect the freedoms not only of our country, but also around the world.

Today many consider America, the land of freedom and opportunity and as a consequence, we are now being overrun with not only legal immigration but also illegal alien migration to our land. In many cases, crossing our borders almost at will. Yes, without question, the take-over of this country, by almost any means necessary, has become the goal of other races of people. It is time the whites of America come to know and understand this.

We as members of the white race willingly faced the hardships of building this country. We were not quitters—nor were our forefathers' crybabies—they did not play the "blame game." Today, I find it amazing that persons of Mexican descent of black descent are now trying to take credit for the building of this nation. Ask them and they will tell you that we stole the borderlands from the Mexicans. Ask many of the descendants of black slavery and they, in their ignorance, will tell you that the blacks built this country.

Yes, in today's world, we have developed a new IBM, the Indians, Blacks and Mexicans who are quick to lay claim to our land and cry foul / Racists when it suits their agenda—the eventual take over of this nation.

In this manner, for the most part, the Indians are, so to speak, passive and docile when it comes to the overthrow of our nation. They have, however, joined the other two races in their ever-increasing demands. That's right, our sports teams cannot be called "Redskins or Braves" and the fans cannot use the "Tomahawk Chop." Makes you wonder; when will they go on the "Warpath" again?

Does it not make you wonder how it is that a great number of former black prisoners have suddenly found religion—the Muslin Religion—the same group of people that were responsible for 9/11/01? Ask yourself, how it is that the Black Panthers have adopted the Muslim Religion? Could they have some hidden agenda? If not, why are they often seen dressed in para-military uniforms and parading in our streets as if they already owned them.

How is it that "Calipso Louie Farra-con" is freely consorting with the enemies of this nation? What is Jesse Jackson doing running around the world acting as though he is, already, an official member of the U.S. Government? What we do not need now is Jessie running around the world talking rap and sucking up to the enemies of our nation. Has he not the brains or the sense to know that he is only being used by these nations. Does he really think he has some power or influence in the world? Now Big Al, our nations first Drugstore Cowboy, was running for the Presidency of this Nation. My oh my, how low can we go? If Clinton is/was our first Black president, one could rightly say, enough is enough—another black president we don't need!

But the real threat to this nation, from within, will come from the Mexican/Hispanic American citizens. In the next two decades, we may be faced with a situation much like Canada experienced with the attempted secession of French speaking Quebec. We already have a large Spanish-speaking population in the Southwestern States, hell bent on turning this nation into a bilingual Spanish-English speaking nation and to eventually control the southern/southwest Border States.

As shown in a report by the American Immigration Control Foundation (AIC) they have: "…Already a militant Hispanic movement headquartered in Los Angeles called Casa Aztlan estimates that within twenty to thirty years they will have enough votes in California, Texas, New Mexico and Arizona to win a secession vote to set up a new Hispanic nation or reunify with Mexico. On 90 percent of the public high school and university campuses in the Southwestern United States there is a group called MEXA. *The preamble to the MEXA constitution states: Chicana/Chicano students of

California must politicize our RAZA (race) and continue the struggle for self-determination of the Chicana/Chicano and the liberation of the nation of Aztlan. Article II, Section 1 states that the "General membership shall consist of any student who accepts, believes and works for the goals and objectives of [MEXZ] including the liberation of Aztlan, meaning self-determination of our people in this 'occupied state' and the physical liberation of our land."

In a California conference entitled "The Immigration Crisis," Dr. Jose Angel Gutierrez, from the University of Texas drew cheers from his audience when he shouted:

Why do they come after us? Because we are fighting as a new Meztizo nation, not to be conquered...we are going to build Aztlan—we are here again...We are millions! Regardless of the outcome in the short term, we have to survive. There is an aging white America; they are not making babies. It is a matter of time. The most preferred minority (blacks) are not making babies, their numbers are declining. Their expectations exceed what they are entitled to. Asians are at our heels, don't get comfortable. You've got to get ready to govern. You must believe that you are entitled to govern. They say you are latinizing Los Angeles—I love it! Aztlan is our homeland! We are here again."

*Until 1997, they called their organization MECHA—Movimiento Estudiantil Chicano de Aztian. Then the spelling of Chicano was changed to Xicano and the movement is now called MEXA.

No one could read this and not come to the conclusion that we have a race of citizens, working from within our country, organizing for the eventual overthrow of this nation. We can be sure that Dr. Gutierrez is not just spouting empty rhetoric. He wants to do for the Mexicans of America what Mexico has done for them—nothing. In his case, he is an ignorant man, but even ignorant people, given such, will answer his call and once again, havoc will rain down on this land

But mark my words: Those that do answer the call will rue the day they did—for only a fool would think that we, the white man, as well as the majority of our citizens—regardless of race—will surrender our country to a bunch of rag-tag upstarts that do not have the brains to realize what they would loose in such a confrontation. But they will remain determined to "screw" us out of part or all of the country. We would be fools not to take them seriously!

"The nation is burdened with the heavy curse on those who come afterwards. The generation before us was inspired by an activism and a naive enthusiasm which we cannot rekindle because we confront tasks of a different kind from those which our fathers faced." Max Weber

Chapter II
Socialism – Tax Slaves

Just as insidious to the overt Mexican threat to the take-over of our nation is the Democrats Socialistic agenda. To support this contention/ belief, I submit the following:

1. In 1898, under the guidance of Eugene Victor Deb, the number one socialist of his time, after a split had occurred in Socialist ranks, the Socialist Democratic Party was founded. In 1900 Deb was the first presidential candidate of the Socialist Democratic Party, commonly called the Socialist Party.

2. In 1860, in the cities of London and New York, the Workingman's (men's) Association was organized by Karl Marx and this organization, in fact, was the genesis of the organized labor movement.

3. One of the founders of the NAACP, W.E.B. Du Bois, a white man, and an avowed Communist, was a strong believer in government control of the people.

From the above, one can readily ascertain that the Democratic Party, the Unions and the NAACP as well had their roots grounded in socialism if not outright communism. As such, under the Democratic Socialistic agenda of today, and with the full support of organized labor and the NAACP, coupled with the Mexican/Hispanic participation in said party. This nation has and will continue to experience the greatest transfer of wealth from the productive to the unproductive members of our society, in its history. If it is allowed to continue, even if the Mexicans were to succeed in their take over attempt, it would probably be a take over of a nation in, at the least, financial disarray and, at the worst, financial ruin.

How can this come to pass? Well, for starters, we need only look to the Democrats and its "Rich against the Poor" political strategy. Yes, it is their "Robin Hood" agenda of "Rob the Rich and give to the Poor" that has, over and over, brought this nation to the brink of financial ruination. One need only to remember history to know that when the Romans tried this under their "Bread and Circuses" policy, it resulted in the fall of the Roman Empire. So, if you think it can't happen here, think again!

In the year 1999 I wrote a self-published book titled: "United we Stand by Diversity we Fall" wherein I wrote a chapter on White Slavery which, in effect, points out how the productive part of society, of which the great majority of people are primarily white citizens and are, if not already, soon to become slaves to ever increasing Government Taxation to support government—welfare—largess—programs. For example, under the "Great Society" programs, we have made a large part of out society dependent on "Big Brother" government.

In a column written by Paul Craig Roberts and published in the Middle America News, June 2000, he wrote:

"Allan Keyes...says that the income tax is a slave tax and that Americans are slaves." He is correct.

A slave is a person who does not own his own labor. After tax, successful Americans retain no more of the income they product than 19th century slaves—and considerable less than medieval serfs...A slave who withheld his labor was likely to be punished. He would be put on short rations or whipped. If one of us today withholds from the IRS, the punishment is more severe—several years in prison.

The slave tax is very expensive in other ways. It takes 6.1 billion hours—more than 3 million man-years—to comply with the slave tax. In dollar terms, it costs us slaves an additional $200 billion to comply with a 2,840 page tax code—more than twice the number of pages as the Bible and more than three times the words."

The federal tax rules interpreting the code come to 46,000 pages…"

And of course, we are all aware, or should be, that the Democratic Political Party is and has always been the party of "Tax and Spend." Yes, the many liberals within this party are more willing to enslave you to high taxes just to appease their "bleeding hearts." Yes, this is also the party that has even initiated action and did, in fact, retroactively tax the dead. The Democrats will follow you to your grave to insure they get your last dime. After all, they need every dime they can get just to appease their constituency.

Quoting again from the aforementioned column:

"…You may say that we Americans are nothing like slaves and that nothing happens to us as long as we do our duty. The same thing can be said about the 19th century slaves. As long as they worked at a reasonable pace, they had room and board and clothes on their backs…"

Given our high rate of taxation, some of our taxpayers are lucky to still have a shirt on their backs—after paying their taxes!

"A government which robs Peter to pay Paul can always depend on the support of Paul." [Or in today's world, on Jose, Jesse and the Union Bosses]. George Bernard Shaw.

Chapter III
Freedom to Want

Speaking before congress on January 6, 1941, President Roosevelt expressed his desire for a world built upon the four freedoms:

The first is freedom of speech and expression – everywhere in the world.

The second is freedom of every person to worship God in his own way – everywhere in the world.

The third is freedom from want – which, translated into world terms, means economic understandings which will secure to every nation a healthy peace time life for it's inhabitants – everywhere in the world.

The fourth is freedom from fear – which translated into world terms, means a world-wide reduction of armaments to such a point and is such a thorough fashion that no nation will be in a position to commit an act of physical aggression against any neighbor – anywhere in the world.

Today, I am sorry to say these dreams have yet to be brought to fruition, neither in the United States – nor anywhere in the world. Looking back, in retrospect, it appears that the four freedoms would appear to have been wishful thinking if not a "Pipe Dream." In fact, today in America, there are many groups within our social structure who are unwilling to accept equality. No, this is not longer good enough for them. They want special/ additional rights over the rest of our society. They have, somehow, come to the conclusion that we, the white man, now owes them more, much more, than other citizens within our country get. It is no longer equality that they seek, but advantage. Let us look at the three groups of citizens referred to in this book, our nations new "IBM" Indians, Blacks, and Mexicans:

INDIANS: They, at least the majority of them, are so dependent on government support that, one could rightly say, they are destined to be wards of our country/government in perpetuity. In our ignorance, we have taken a once proud people and reduced them to a life of dependence.

When we, as a nation, as a people, first encountered the "Indians", we mistakenly assumed that they were an indigenous race of people to this land. Not so, this continent, America, is a rarity and is the only continent on this planet Earth that did not have a truly native people. The fact that they were here first did not give them the right to lay ownership to a whole continent of which they never touched or left their footprints on. We know that they arrived here by a land bridge from Asia, as Nomads. Their goal was to neither explore nor settle this land but to follow the migrating herds and reap the bounty of this land that nature provided.

The Indians are also held out as the only Native Americans. Not True! If you are born in America, regardless of the date and time, you are a Native American. In short, the Indians, because they arrived here first, are no more or solely a Native American than those that were born here afterwards are. If you were born here, you are just as much a Native American as they are.

Again, it must be stated that the Indians, on what little land they occupied, that their mere presence did not give them ownership to all the land. We as a nation and as a race fought them for the land and won the war. The vanquished—the Indians— lost the war and were relegated to a space in our nations history. We treated them with compassion and provided them with a lifetime of security. No other nation has ever done as much.

BLACKS – As we are all aware, their race of people, or the great majority of them, arrived on the American Continent as slaves. Slaves that were sold by their own people, in the world slave markets. Was slavery wrong—Yes! But it was a market founded in the African as well as in the Arabic nations. The white man, like all peoples of the world of that time, participated in the slave trade—they did not originate it—the Black Slave Trade.

The blacks sold to/in American Colonies were, if being a slave can be so designated, the lucky ones. Those slaves sold in many other parts of the world were automatically doomed. If can be factually shown that the American slaves, of all the slaves sold throughout the world, had the highest survival rate of all. Not only that, but their descendants have prospered in America beyond anything their ancestors could have ever dreamed of.

Did they suffer hardships and indignities in/at the hands of the slavers and slave owners? The answer would have to be a resounding yes. But throughout history, all mankind suffered in one way or another—a lot worse than the American slaves.

Was their life better for their coming to America as slaves, or worse? Had they stayed in Africa, as slaves, would they have lived long enough to even have descendents—I doubt it! Still, today, the descendents born out of the African slave trade are wont to blame only the white man for the acts of slavery when, in fact, slavery had its roots in the African Nations. The white man did not even participate in the black slave trade until early in the 17th century.

It is the white man that can also be considered the first race of people to initiate action to end slavery. Today, in many parts/countries on North and South Africa, slavery is still running rampant and, if anything more abhorrent.

Today, much of the black leadership in America, one would have to think, are nothing but cheap profiteers and racial opportunists. Of the four freedoms annunciated by Franklin D. Roosevelt, the one they seem to like the most, in a fashion, is the freedom from Want. However, they have misconstrued this freedom to mean: FREEDOM TO WANT!

Yes, for many years, their cry was for equal rights and finally they got them. Did this pacify them? The answer is a resounding NO! Today, they no longer cry for equal rights but more and more rights—rights by which only their race can benefit, such as: Quotas, Affirmative Action and much, much more.

In addition, they want the right to riot in the streets each time a decision goes against them either in the courts or in other ways not to their liking. No other race of people in this nation has been so granted the right to randomly violate our laws. They are quick to speak of the many perceived wrongs they have had to endure, but they are very slow to recognize the many advantages of the good they have reaped.

Now, in addition – we have many groups of these black citizens – wanting to pick, further, the pockets of the white man; demanding that they receive compensation (reparations) for the labors of their ancestors. This nation, as a whole, did not profit from slavery and in the southern states where slavery was practiced they have, over all these many years, suffered an economic shortfall. For years, they have had lower wages and a loss/delay in establishing a manufacturing base.

Since 1964, this nation has contributed trillions of dollars to improve the "general welfare" of the blacks, only to be met with cries for more and more. This despite the fact that a great majority of such money has been squandered or ripped off by the very people it was supposed to help.

However, to me, the most troubling thing that is now happening in this nation is the many black convicts coming out of prison as supposedly "Religious Converts." And to what religion—the "Muslim" religion. I find it strange that so many of them are converting to a religious group that has been, as they claim, misunderstood and that they do not support the terrorists or terrorism. Still each day, as of late, that goes by, we hear something of either their complicity or to support some group or person involved in planning or attempting to do harm to this country.

I am also left to wonder how it is that, in recent years; we are finding many of the black leadership within this nation giving support and comfort to our present day enemies. Seems they have enough trouble in many of our inter-city black communities where they could, perhaps, do some good: as opposed to running around the world as if they, somehow, had the power to do any good. First, they should try to clean up their act on the home front.

MEXICANS/HISPANICS – In regards to some citizens, within this race, they are looking to change the meaning of the First Freedom— freedom of speech as well as the Third Freedom— freedom from want. If they had their way, it would be freedom of speech but only in "Spanish" and also, they would like to have the freedom not from want but to "want more."

Basically, I think that there are all too many people, within this race, who still think that they once owned a part of this country and hope to somehow, someway, take at least that part of this nation back! This would be a folly of gigantic miscalculation and a great loss to this nation. For those of a mind that would think that such a course of action would bring them victory, or even minor advantage should think long and hard. Remember, we have in our nations history crossed this path before, however, it was to save the Union, not divide it. In such a conflict, as indicated, to take away a part of this country, one could be sure to realize that there would be hell to pay for those who might be foolish enough to try!

"We must remember that any oppression, any injustice, any hatred, is a wedge designed to attack our civilization." Franklin D. Roosevelt.

Chapter IV
Racial Pride

As a white man I have been fortunate to, throughout my life, have a close and friendly relationship with African American, as well as Hispanic/Mexican Americans. They are, to my mind, some of the most fun-loving and loyal friends I have ever had. These people, of both races, once your friend, are always your friend. Like any race of people, there are good as well as bad. Today, thanks to the media, it is all too frequently that what is shown on television is only the bad and, as a consequence, they are being stereotyped as "the root of all evil." Not so! The great majority of them are honest, hard working, productive citizens and loyal Americans who, in the main, contribute to this nation as equals, asking only for equal not special rights, no more, no less. This they deserve. This they should have. Today, and rightly so, they have organizations such as the NAACP, CORE,

LULAC, RAZA UNIDA and others, to champion their causes. However, and all too frequently, the KKK and skin heads are held out as representative of the white man's feelings and beliefs. I resent this! They are no more representatives of the white race than the drive-by shooters or car jackers are of their respective races. I guess that we, the white people, can share some of the blame for this mischaracterization. As a race we have not felt it necessary to band together in such a manner. We have always dealt with our problems as individuals; however, maybe the time has come for a change. We, the white people, in order to preserve our tights, might look, as the other races have, to forming a group to represent us as a "block" to insure our needs and desires are also addressed. Also, maybe we should use the lessons of the Blacks- massive protests sometimes serve a need/cause!

The white man as no other race of people on this earth, has contributed the most to the advancement of all mankind. He can, among all races, stand tall and with is head held high. Am I saying that white man is smarter – no. What I am saying is that for some reason, the white race used their innate talents – talents possessed by all races – to better advantage. This cannot be denied nor disproved; it is a factual statement. In my research for this book and in trying to be fair, I, time after time, could only find white representation in the forefront of the sciences, arts, exploration and so forth. Yes, the other races are represented in these fields and have made many contributions, but not comparable to their numbers. Don't ask me why this is so – I don't know – but I can speculate and, in doing so, I can only come up with, perhaps, the reasons for the white man's better use of his talents is his willingness to accept responsibility for his actions. As a result/consequence he is more willing to take a chance to succeed and or to fail. I am not stating this as a fact; it is only my reasoned answer to the question posed. However, my answer as to why the white man has progressed far beyond his numbers is, I feel, his personal self-esteem. Today the African Americans and Hispanics are too busy playing the blame-game. Yes they have, like all peoples on this earth, suffered some indignities; dwelling on them serves them no good. Remember, in building this nation, the white people also faced untold hardships and many difficulties, but they persevered. For example:

The Pilgrims had to face hardship.

The men at Valley Forge had to face hardship.

The men at Gettysburgh had to face hardship.

The men, in all the wars since our founding, had to face hardship.

The settlers and homesteaders had to face hardship.

As you can see, the white founders of this country faced many hardships along the way to building this great nation. They did not pause to place blame but got on with their lives.

When the Mayflower docked, it was white Anglo-Saxon Europeans who got off the ship at Plymouth Rock.

It was the Continental Army, comprised of white men that fought and won this nation's freedoms and liberties.

It was the white man, during the Civil War, who was willing to fight his brother(s) to insure equality and freedom for all.

Yes, it was the white man who pioneered this country, settled it and developed its lands and resources, because of this he, the white man, is its founder and the builder of this great nation, the greatest country in the world. No one can deny or take exception to the truth of this statement, We, as the African Americans and Hispanics want to champion their heritage, also want to champion our heritage and, in my way of thinking, no other race has more right to do so than the white race. This is evidenced every day; people from all around the globe are trying and many dying, to get into this country. No other nation but the United States of America can make this claim. I say this not to disparage against any race of people but only to show absolute pride in my race.

"The only equality is in the cemetery." German Proverb

Chapter V
Government

"We the people of the United States, in order to form a more perfect union, establish justice, insure domestic tranquillity, provide for the common defense, promote the general welfare, and secure the blessings of liberty to ourselves to out posterity, do ordain and establish the 'Constitution for the United States of America'."

The end of the colonial period in 1776, meant the end of the only governmental system the colonists had known. After the Declaration of Independence, a new government system had to be formed and this, in time, developed into the Constitution of the United States which was formally adopted in 1789.

Our system is unique because it is federal – both State as will as the federal government have overlapping systems, each of which has authority in some areas but not in others. For example:

States have no authority in foreign affairs; the U.S. Government has no right to tax real property. Over the years, since 1789, we have seen a gradual growth of power in Federal Government, at the expense of states rights. It is only now that our citizens are beginning to look at, with apprehension, that sooner or later the states will have little or no power. At the same time, people are becoming more and more disillusioned with the national governments" inability to solve many of todays" problems as well as those of the future.

Our forefathers, having come from and been ruled by an oppressive government attempted to prevent the federal government usurping the states constitutions by adding 10 amendments to the federal constitution which we call the "Bill of Rights," also known as your "inalienable rights" which are:

1st Amendment – Your right to freedom of speech, press, religion, and assembly.

2nd Amendment – The right to keep and bear arms.

3rd Amendment – Quartering troops.

4th Amendment – Unreasonable search and seizure.

5th Amendment – Right to a Grand Jury indictment, double jeopardy; right to compulsory process and right to counsel.

6th Amendment - Right to an impartial jury, right to confront your accuser, right to compulsory process and right to counsel.

7th Amendment – Right to civil jury.

8th Amendment – Cruel and unusual punishment.

9th Amendment – Rights retained by the people – privacy.

10th Amendment – Powers reserved to the States.

Today, we have 26 amendments to the constitution; however, the 14th amendment has been frequently used by the courts to bring about many changes in the American legal system which, for the most part, have taken place since the end of the Civil War. As you will see, and it is interesting to note, that Section 1 of the 14th amendment is directed against the states, whereas the first 10 amendments are directed against the federal government. Section 1 of the 14th amendment reads:

"All persons born or naturalized in the United States and subject to the jurisdiction therein, are citizens of the United States and the State wherein they reside. No State shall make or enforce any law which shall abridge the privilege of immunity of citizens in the United States; nor shall any State deprive any person of life, liberty, or property, without due process of law; nor deny to any person within it's jurisdiction the equal protection of the law."

So, in essence, we have two principal sources of protection against any violation of our basic individual rights; your states rights and the laws of the United States. In the years, since the adoption of the 14th Amendment, this amendment has been used more and more to control the actions of the state governments. Today, the federal government, whose power was once so feared, has become the government of last resort. Although the 14th Amendment has done much, along with the Bill of Rights, for persons asserting their civil rights and liberties, it has also been one of the main tools to asserting federal control over the states. Today, our state's rights are frequently being abused through the use of mandates by the many governmental bureaucracies.

Basically a mandate as defines in the dictionary gives a degree of dictatorial power(s) to the federal government. According to the Heritage Dictionary, these two words: mandate and dictate are synonymous; as illustrated:

Dictate: 2. To issue (a command order, etc..) authoritatively.

Mandate; 1. An authoritative command or instruction.

Call it a mandate if you want, but we have lost a great many states rights by allowing our federal government to dictate to the states by the many federal bureaucracies; i.e., the Alcohol, Tobacco and Firearms Agency (ATF), the Environmental Protection Agency (EPA), the Fish and Wildlife Service and so on.

Our States rights as will as our constitutional rights are slowly being eroded and left to the federal bureaucrats dictatorial ways; we are on the way to a socialist government at best or at it's worst, rule by a world government. How can or could this happen? Easily, not only are our states rights being lost but our individual rights are daily being challenged, i.e. freedom of religion, the right to bear arms, our property rights, water rights and so on. We, as a once proud people and rich nation have, under the liberal democratic control of the nation's purse strings over the past forty years, gone from the richest nation in the world to the biggest debtor nation in the world. Where did this money/wealth go? It supposedly went to the needy by virtue of and through our over generous welfare programs. These liberal programs have done in 40 years – through the Great Society Program – what no other nation could do, bring the United States to its financial knees. Who of us 30 years ago could have imagined that so much of the wealth of this country could have been so wasted? Today our welfare system is that great "sucking sound" that Ross Perot was hearing. It is draining our country financially dry. Can anyone in their right mind say that our welfare program has been a success? If they can, will they please explain to me why, today, the cry for more money, more money, more money is still heard from these social engineers. If the programs had been successful we would not be hearing these continued cries for help. Today the Black Caucus will not vote for any bill that does not have some "pork" in it for their constituency. Its no wonder Farrakhan hates the Jews; the Jews don't like pork. Think about it! If our government is allowed to continue, unchallenged on its present course we, as Americans, will all be the losers. We must not and cannot let this happen. We must do all within our power and particularly through our vote, to insure this country remains democratic and free! Today we are on a collision course with socialism, and once it is imbedded into our society we will be on the slippery slope to ruination, resulting in the loss of our rights and freedoms as granted to us under the constitution. We must stop this madness now.

"Violence has no constitutional sanction; and every government from the beginning has moved against it. But where grievances pile high and most elected spokesmen represent the Establishment, violence may be the only effectie response." Wiliam O.Doul

"There must be what Mr. Gladstone many years ago called a "blessed act of oblivion." We must all turn our backs upon the horrors of the past. We must look to the future. We cannot afford to drag forward across the years that are yet to come the hatreds and revenges which have sprung from the injuries of the past." Winston Churchill

Reference

African and Africans – By Paul Bohannan and Phillip Curtain
Africans in History – By Basil Davidson
At any Cost – By Bill Sammon
The Indian Frontier of the American West 1846 – 1890 – By Robert M. Utley
The West – By Geoffrey C. Ward
Tribal Wars of the Southern Plains – By Stan Hoig
Selling our Birthright – By Joseph L. Daleiden
Race and Culture – By Thomas Sowell
United we Stand by Diversity we Fall (self-published) – By James J. Dobranich, Sr.

In addition:

The New York Times Almanacs
The Random House Encyclopedia (electronic edition)
Reader's Digest

www.ingramcontent.com/pod-product-compliance
Lightning Source LLC
Chambersburg PA
CBHW020238290526
45784CB00003B/1026